ON THE WATER

Water Skiing

by Rachel Grack

BLASTOFF! READERS, AN IMPRINT OF BELLWETHER MEDIA BY FLUTTERBEE

Blastoff! Readers are carefully developed by literacy experts to build reading stamina and move students toward fluency by combining standards-based content with developmentally appropriate text.

Level 1 provides the most support through repetition of high-frequency words, light text, predictable sentence patterns, and strong visual support.

Level 2 offers early readers a bit more challenge through varied sentences, increased text load, and text-supportive special features.

Level 3 advances early-fluent readers toward fluency through increased text load, less reliance on photos, advancing concepts, longer sentences, and more complex special features.

★ **Blastoff! Universe**

Reading Level

Blastoff! Beginners — Grade K

Blastoff! Readers — Grades 1–3

Blastoff! Discovery — Grade 4

This edition first published in 2027 by Bellwether Media, Inc.

For information regarding permission, write to Bellwether Media, Inc., Attention: Permissions Department, 3500 American Blvd W, Suite 150, Bloomington, MN 55431.

Library of Congress Cataloging-in-Publication Data is available at www.loc.gov or upon request from the publisher.

ISBN: 9798898800628 (hardcover)
ISBN: 9798898801861 (ebook)

Editor: Kieran Downs   Series Designer: Josh Brink   Designer: Laura Sowers

Printed in the United States of America, North Mankato, MN.

Table of Contents

Zipping Over Water

Water skiing is a water sport. Motorboats pull people on skis.

People water ski on lakes, rivers, and oceans.

Top Place to Water Ski

Winter Haven, Florida, United States

There are many kinds of water skis. Beginners often use **combination skis**.

Some skis are better for tricks.
Others are better for turns.

Boats pull skiers with ski ropes. Skiers hold the rope handle while skiing.

Spotters watch water skiers to make sure they stay safe.

spotters

Water skiers must wear life jackets. Some skiers wear gloves for a better **grip**.

Bindings keep skiers' feet on the skis.

What Water Skiers Need

Getting Started on Water Skiing

Water skiers often begin on two skis. This makes it easier to get up.

Some skiers can get up on one ski.

Many water skiers start in the water. They pull their knees close to their chest.

They keep their ski tips **parallel** in front of them.

Skiers hold the rope
between their skis.

The boat pulls them out of the water. They straighten their legs and stand up.

Slalom skiers do fast turns. They cross the **wake** and ski around **buoys**.

Water Skiing Moves

start

turns

jumps

tricks

Show skiers perform tricks.
They do jumps, spins, and flips.

Go Water Skiing!

Skiers use water skiing hand signals. They **communicate** with the spotter.

Ski flags let other boaters know a skier is in the water. Go water skiing!

Glossary

bindings—straps that hold a skier's feet onto water skis

buoys—floating objects that mark locations in water

combination skis—a pair of water skis that can be used to double ski or slalom ski

communicate—to send and receive information

grip—a tight hold

parallel—extending side by side in straight lines without touching

slalom—related to a type of water skiing where a skier does turns around buoys in the water

spotters—people in a boat who watch the skier

wake—the track of waves behind a motorboat

To Learn More

AT THE LIBRARY

Catena, Melissa. *Water Safety.* Minneapolis, Minn.: Jump!, 2025.

Grack, Rachel. *Kitesurfing.* Minneapolis, Minn.: Bellwether Media, 2027.

Grack, Rachel. *Wakeboarding.* Minneapolis, Minn.: Bellwether Media, 2027.

ON THE WEB

FACTSURFER

Factsurfer.com gives you a safe, fun way to find more information.

1. Go to www.factsurfer.com.
2. Enter "water skiing" into the search box and click .
3. Select your book cover to see a list of related content.

Index

The images in this book are reproduced through the courtesy of: Kozlik, front cover (top); Chaos/ Getty Images, front cover (bottom); master1305, pp. 3, 8, 13; leeds, p. 4; Cassiohabib, pp. 4-5; Billy F Blume Jr, p. 5; Brocreative, p. 6; Alex Bogatyrev, pp. 6-7, 19 (tricks); MrPants, pp. 8-9; jentakespictures, pp. 10-11; PatrycjaLoeppky, p. 11; auremar, pp. 12-13; Uncleasam, p. 14; Marc Dufresne, pp. 14-15; ArtBoyMB, p. 16; Fotokostic, pp. 16-17; milkovasa, p. 18; jeffstrauss, pp. 18-19; wanderluster, p. 19 (start); Sokirlov, p. 19 (turns); Lifestyle Imagery/ Alamy, p. 19 (jumps); CroMary, pp. 20-21; Real Sports Photos, p. 21; Cerae, p. 23.